Also by Robert Milton Ph.D.

TIPS --- The Imaginative Parent Succeeds

Hole in the Soul (fiction)

The Unspoken (fiction)

The True Believers --- The Golden Age of Terrorism

The Reach (fiction)

The Flexxible Brain --- Bigger Better Brain via Neuro-Nastics

Woman Aware --- eliminate religious creed - emancipate women

\|\|\|\|\|

NUMINOUS MIRRORS
EMPIRICAL SCIENCE --- THE POETRY OF NATURE

ROBERT MILTON Ph.D.

authorHOUSE®

AuthorHouse™
1663 Liberty Drive
Bloomington, IN 47403
www.authorhouse.com
Phone: 1-800-839-8640

© 2013 Robert Milton Ph.D.. All rights reserved.

No part of this book may be reproduced, stored in a retrieval system, or transmitted by any means without the written permission of the author.

Published by AuthorHouse 10/17/2013

ISBN: 978-1-4918-2651-5 (sc)
ISBN: 978-1-4918-2652-2 (e)

Library of Congress Control Number: 2013918562

Any people depicted in stock imagery provided by Thinkstock are models, and such images are being used for illustrative purposes only.
Certain stock imagery © Thinkstock.

This book is printed on acid-free paper.

Because of the dynamic nature of the Internet, any web addresses or links contained in this book may have changed since publication and may no longer be valid. The views expressed in this work are solely those of the author and do not necessarily reflect the views of the publisher, and the publisher hereby disclaims any responsibility for them.

DEDICATED TO

The wondrous gift of 'being' for a short time
"…the lucky ones…"

CONTENTS

Introduction 1

Naturalism 5

If - No Doubt 7

Mind Strolling 9

Always – Blasphemy 11

Love's Vacuum 13

Dreaming 15

Genesis 17

Tree of Life 19

Virus Buddies 21

Women Waiting 23

Consciousness 25

Moral Terror 29

Passionate Life 31

Heroes—Ask Alice 33

Abstraction Anathema 35

Define Me 39

I Abhor	41
The Real Danger	43
Intentions	45
Talent and Genius	47
Wave Fable	49
Ocean Waves Metaphor	51
H_2O	55
Placebo	57
Free Will	61
Wrongly They Say	63
Poetry	67
Where I'd Like to Go	69
Peril of Risk	71
Dance with a Shadow	73
Yellow Cub	75
Blind Dating	77
What's the Point	81
Metaphysics	83
Sincere	87

I Don't Know the Meaning	89
I Don't Know How to Describe	91
Gray Questions	93
Brain Evolution	95
Megatropolis	97
Yosemite Night Sky	99
Buddhism	101
Existential Pool Blather	105
The Deep Inside	107
"Good ol' Days"	109
Dawn sans Heroes	115
Dawkins "the lucky ones"	116

INTRODUCTION

I have wondered:

What is this thing called, in ancient as well as modern times, a "mystical experience" or sometimes just plain "faith"?

Is metaphysics a mere soothing consolation for our flawed human existence?

Why and how does our evolved brain trick us into thinking we are not animals?

What is the role of women, the superior gender, in our contemporary world?

How do obsessions ("belief" "hope" and "faith") continue to hold our attention? Or keep us distracted — depending on your point of view?

And of course, "Love" — The ultimate human desire, aspiration and mystery.

Childhood is for most — it was for me — a time of fable, fairy tales, and fabulous magic! In my mind, I was completely satisfied when correlation was called causation and when told "God moves in mysterious ways." I considered that was a factual answer and not simply a way of dismissing additional inquiry. Further, I was in total awe at every seemingly undiscoverable (not yet understood) phenomenon. Magic indeed!

Then, it happened! A grown up person usurped my body and my brain. In rapid succession, some beliefs were replaced with some facts. Logic and a lot of questioning came into being — and more recently morphed into skepticism. When I read that Einstein said, "The most incomprehensible thing in this universe is — it's all comprehensible"— that did it. I knew that bona fide "real" consensually validated answers were available; it was just up to me to search and find them.

The traditional societal and religious impressions of my youth gradually faded in a measured manner while facing the distinctive facts that university studies of history and science offered. I admit that today I live in a state of almost constant awe, primarily because I have been blessed with a curious mind and have an almost insatiable need to turn over stones rather than just take another's best guess at what might be revealed. Curiosity then, remains my aperture to spirituality. Yes, wonder, amazement and awe are relentlessly presented to me as I skeptically ask questions and find myself standing in a state of "spiritual awe" as one answer after another unfolds revealing still more questions.

Even as questions invade, I know now for sure, there are not enough days of sunlight left for me to discover all my answers to the unending stream of questions coming my way. My willingness to say YES to the quest for openness, is for me, even at this late stage, what intimacy with *the other* truly means. To grasp, even for a second, the synergistic miracle of *being* in love is like experiencing a Doppler sound. One can encounter and embrace its coming, arriving and departing. (This is easy to say, not so easy to do.) I have learned, even while watching the sun setting on my life, that it better to feel the experience even in its departing mode — as every experience must — than to support the regrets of what might have been. My life has been punctuated with hundreds of goodbyes — each one seemingly more poignant than the one before. Yet, I relish saying hello even while knowing goodbye will follow. All of us must say goodbye to everything eventually. On the last page of this book Dr. Richard Dawkins has still another take on life and death.

But I still wonder about the relevance of traditional "beliefs" and so called "New Age" views in a contemporary world. Even as our world is illuminated and described by evidence and facts rather than fear of the unknown and mythology, there remains what appears to be an ambiguity in American culture.

Even today, I question — if faith is an obsession — what is poetry? Is Science the poetry of nature? Or is it as Yeats said: "We make out of the quarrel with others, rhetoric, but of the quarrel with ourselves, poetry." Since science is but one new question after another, it too, is a kind of self-quarrel. When is enough ever enough?

The poems that follow are, in my mind, more questions, self-quarrels and a relatively benign attempt at offering to myself, partial illumination to a few, very few, of my mind's ever surfacing questions.

Looking for a way to define my "beliefs" I turned from the usual and oft misunderstood terms: agnostic and atheist, to nature herself. I am a naturalist.

NATURALISM

When self-definitions
Of the 'me' – 'myself' - and 'I'
come calling –
knocking on my cerebral door
requiring – no — demanding an answer—
Who? Why? and How?

When old limp rags 'Metaphysic' or 'Atheist'
won't do because they're rancid
and bicker with definition baggage
from which bone weary arguments
and tiresome philosophies
are hone and gown.

In place of *faith* obsessions
Ms Nature's discernible!
and she opens lightness
and the glorious stuff
of authentic words like poetry
and promising metaphors

In fact, I often,
with curiosity leading the way,
turn without a second thought
into the warming light of Natures'
awe-inspiring curtsy
revealing her petticoat luminosity

Clearly I am of Nature
Why would I not
seek the ordinary natural world
and her creation:
Naturalism itself
to define myself ?

Satire is the use of humor, irony, and exaggeration, to expose human stupidity or vices, particularly in the context of contemporary politics and/or religion.

Satire was a late discovery for me and when it erupts, I find it is often mistaken for cynicism.
Sigh.

IF - NO DOUBT

If - man did not make god
In his image
Then <u>everything</u> would be sacred and holy
No doubt

If - poetry could tell the whole truth
And language itself, not lie
Then words would be more than enough
No doubt

If - the distant celestial astrals
Could predict anything substantial
Then everything would be known and understood
No doubt

If - one of the many bibles
IS the truth of God
Then everything in that land is peace, milk and honey
No doubt

If - there were actually a heaven in the sky
Where saint sans sinner abide
Then in truth: it's the foremost apartheid
No doubt

If – words from above are factual fable
Or mean anything at all
Then we may overlook the joy of finding out.
Yes doubt!

Pantoum, a class exercise, is composed of a series of quatrains; the second and fourth lines of each stanza are repeated as the first and third lines of the next. The meaning of lines can change when they are repeated although the words remain exactly the same:

MIND STROLLING EXERCISE IN PALM'S SPRINGS

As I stroll in the noon day heat
While breathing the stifling hotness
I am burning but not up
Holding memories' noir shade
While breathing the stifling hotness
My mind holds a shadow tenderly
Holding memories' noir shade
Feeling its softness amid firmness
While breathing the stifling hotness
I am burning but not up
My mind holds a shadow tenderly
As I stroll in the noon day heat

The following poem is an effort to contrast two relatively common human temperaments or "Modes Operandi" — one needing specific answers, the other, content to live with open-ended questing. Can we or do we dare, identify ourselves?

Always and Forever
BUNSEN BURNERS, AND BLASPHEMIES

- Science & sacrament
may both breathe free
- Spirit we may feel,
while atoms we may see

- Bubbling beakers
flash-drives recast
- detailed empiricism
takes mythology to task

- Physics now minus
metaphysics, quietly arrives
- Bunsen burners energize
as do math and zip drives

- Experiment minus fables
announced as a houseguest
- Lacking the magic tales
believers must protest!

- They say: "Not by bread alone
but a proper spirit fest
- With only quests & questions,
science fails our test

-Without conclusive answers
we are obliged to mock!"
-Yet knowing science's duty
is to seek, track and stalk

- <u>Always</u> - real Science
is devoid of final talk
- or mythical mystical answers
to calm a believing flock

- <u>Forever</u> - adamant believers ridicule
the suggestions & propositions
- because Science only offers implications
and questions of infinite exception

Numinous Mirrors ♦ 11

In life we recurrently we feel loss and coupled with loss there is often a feeling of regret.
To know and then take love for granted is a profound description of regret. The following poem is yet another description:

LOVE'S VACUUM

I have felt the clinch of love
and its biting sting
But life without love
is not worth mentioning
Love can be next to fatal
Impersonal, yet desirable
I am liberal when in-love
Detrimental fits the glove
Animal with a brain so unfair
Avowing "I'm devoted and aware"
But my still fickle capriciousness
births a glance to one elsewhere

So I've searched the social swirl
and the whorls of the hot vortex
I've fretted, fumed, and sought
felt the holy warmth of sacred sex
And journeyed on as is my lot
from suspected sin to redemption.
Tell me then cleanly, clearly
I beg, what is Love's cost?
Where is payment to be found
for feelings so easily lost?

I can feel love's embrace
and then too readily sing
frilly love songs with idyllic lace
that deny the heartache it also brings
But vacuum's neither of my mind
to embrace nor in a body chaste
Yet, In misty distances I clearly see
my own final harvest comes in haste

Thomas Mann was said to write the un-writeable, express the un-expressible In his novel, Doctor Faustus, he allegedly pulled off an empathetic portrayal of good and evil by recasting the Faustus story in modern times. One character, Leverkuhn, studies frozen crystals forming on a farmhouse windowpane. Metaphorically he explains, if they were just symmetrical crystals, regular, and mathematical they would be "good" but these "rude and insolent" crystals dishonestly impersonate the vegetable world fern fronds. Question: Do the crystals mimic fern fronds or do the fronds mimic the crystals? The conclusion: Nature and science, man and woman, can dream the same synergistic dream.

DREAMING

Akin to our night dreams
Nature too ascends out of chaos
Selects meticulous order — messy mysteries
His trivial dream, Her famed dream: The same dream

We dream symmetrical spiels
Sparkling crystals strictly precise
Still sassily imitate biology's fern fronds
Randomness – exactness: The same dream

In the beginning a dream
Brought forth light and darkness
And by some stasis and much flux
That dream, our dream: The same dream

The dream of gas and dust
Gaia's globe of simple molecules
And some 25 thousand miles round
Nature and luck dreamed: The same dream

We dream - I awake - a world ends
A crawling caterpillar naps. A world ends
A butterfly now emerges a new world begins
Beginning and end – now forever: The same dream

In order to say " hello" one must be able to say "goodbye."
Accounting for human beginnings is of necessity a way of accounting for human endings.
Genesis is a story of hello and goodbye.
Being able to say "goodbye" is necessary before one is able to say "hello".
Without the coalition of Hello and Goodbye, relationships become fictional roles — just acting.
An obvious example — parenthood. The successful parent is able to release.
The synergism of hello is goodbye

GENESIS

Hello
in one beginning
Life met Death and thus
appeared the wondrous words
of our inaugural Eden story
containing more than capricious scrawls
of arbitrary rules for muddled mankind.
These enchanting yet ambiguous words,
born of ageless story telling
from fragile peasant hearths
to ornate castle throne rooms
like magic alchemy potions and hex signs.
They cast spells and also curses.
The expressions of Eden purloin literal power
Like Ali Baba opening a covert closet door
with an accidental abracadabra incantation
In the day that thou eat
Thou shall surely die
And die we do!
Goodbye…

The story of EDEN'S TREE OF LIFE has cast a spell of impotence over human rational thought for two thirds of Earth's inhabitants. One interpretation of this story, more than any other, set the tone for dualistic human interaction.

THE TREE OF LIFE IS WHOLENESS

Singular scintillating falling leafs
fleetingly finding a glorious reprieve
Colors afire, then deaths freeze
floating downward hence return
to terra's living roiling dusty urn

Absent judgment, all trees sing
   only what natural cycles bring
      and the oneness of all things
         blending late winter with spring

Eden's Tree, gave fruit to gentle folk
But stone studded kitschy caps invoke
a curse. They defined evil poison oak
divided good from bad - thus sin awoke
HE spoke: "accuse the accursed womenfolk!"

Separate poetry from the throb of word
   As disconnected life from death is absurd
      To untie heaven from hell is wrong
         clerics deign sing nature's natural song

Holy whole of cycles may say
written truth's the potent way
but woman's words held sway:
Live today! There's magic in play
Bad/good apples — now cliché

Eat of dualism, divide, disarrange
   breathings' cycle becomes estranged
      Inhale, exhale – one god-sent - one malevolent
         Darkness benighted, day-ness ignited-

Deny the eternal cycle - repudiate
   then expound the meaning of evil
      Inhale – exhale — eat — defecate,
         Spell LIVE backwards & participate
Reiterate: The tree of life is — life's wholeness

Almost daily I receive Emails revealing contemporary thought. Some of it is silly, some serious and scientific, some political analysis — much is critique. The majority however, is humorous. But that being said, most of the time, the Emails carry metaphorical messages of daily relevance.
The following is no exception.
I made use of the humor attribute to elaborate the concepts. I think it may call attention to basic rules of our living with our ubiquitous invisible world.

VIRUSES BUDDIES AND THE LIKE (OR DISLIKE)

Invisible deadly, viral nano-monsters invade my tiny cell pagodas:
Sign says: "*under new management*" Ford now fabricates Toyotas!

Sneaky Virus invades - occupies my body. Out! Out! Damn bug I say.
Virus replies: "you're not in charge! My fever - my sweat - hold sway"

Infectious microbes skulk in; nuzzle and snuggle into soggy soma compost
Doc orders, "anti-biotic for this creep!" It complains: "you're not a good host!"

Two more bacteria quietly slip through my immune system gaffe.
"Get out, out, damn microbe spots!" I demand. "Can't, we are staph!"

From out the googolplex eternal cosmos an infrared photon spree
And from the wave/particles an epiphany: "Is it <u>hot</u> in here or is it just me?"

Then I think I see the mysterious neutrino goo
Abruptly then, it announces: "just passing through"

Schrodinger's cat strolls into purview
And doesn't ....

Homo sapiens like deadly germs invade gorgeous Gaia's spacecraft
Like viruses seek and demand death rather than requiring a life raft

The *sapiens dominate, creep, crawl, ingest, and shun*
Deny heated global death & repudiate over-population

Elected viral carnivores settle in the DC capital — no cares
in glee publicize their greed and toxic political nightmares

(Enthused by anonymous Email received June 2012)

The following is an attempt to summarize a three act Broadway play entitled THE WAITING ROOM.
Three views of women reacting within their individual male dominated cultural constraints becomes the focus of this sad, ironic play.

WHAT ARE YOU WAITING FOR?

Quip: Women waiting to die? Berated - hated while waiting,
  A modern plaque says: THE WAITING ROOM - For HIS belated?
    Broadway play reveals - Three iconic women - HIS-story dates
      Symbolic women totter on stage, kill time in: "The Room to Wait"

First act: queasy American waits - silicone bags leak
Second act: woman waits on a restricting Victorian street,
unyielding corsets aggravate, as a 'moral' man sneaks a peek.
Third act: Chinese woman waits with tightly bound (rotting) feet.

First act: American men infatuated by fêted big breast fixation.
  A style-sick chic American society venerates boob fascination.
    Twiggy bodies, bulimic diets HIS-story: A pubescent addiction
      The waiting beat persists – morbidly steals another generation

Second act: Insecure Victorian men require ovaries replaced
Why? Her longing: Mind stimulation. (Instead she gains wasp waist)
Predacious males end education pining – her '<u>hysteria</u>' exchanged
Resolution: "<u>Hyster</u>-Ectomy" a searing slash pacifies HIS sick taste

(Then Third view of Asian tradition sans logic) HE of course, insists
 stylishly small peds: Visual metaphor, always HIS gods must dictate
 The fiction: Small feet assert leisurely life for a bound stooped wife
 HE smugly boasts *conspicuous consumption* as HIS Asian life.

Then HE complains, objecting to her slow prolonged death gait
Killing time! Women capitulate - accept the weighty mania of wait
Waiting must look effortless for women, an unsolicited mandate
(Sperm to worm - Womb to tomb) in vain women did & do repudiate

Everywhere HE builds aggregate intact rooms called WAITING
  Waiting rooms, HE says, equate to Dining, Living or placating
    HIS construct: rooms for each - increasingly and ever frustrating.
      Undoubtedly *practice* to implement first quip: women die *waiting*.

Numinous Mirrors ♦ 23

One Summer I spent a month at Esalen Institute in Big Sur taking various classes. One of my instructors suggested the word "maybe" be inserted as a part of my oft-repeated soliloquies. (resolute rants) When the poetry instructor asked the class to write a poem containing ambivalence about a current interest — I attempted to write about Brain Science and "consciousness, and the science of hearing and seeing."
I later discovered he meant a relationship with another person about whom we felt ambivalent. Yes, my face was red when I read to the class and the instructor said, "Eh? Maybe ... it's just me ... but I don't get it!"

MAYBE you'll get it?

SALUTE TO CONSCIOUSNESS –

Some-**one** - the cognomen 'consciousness' resides in my head
    but scientific scans decide She/He/It's not me - it's said
        they say Science measured it and old ideas shed
But in my head some-times-fear-times-dread-times- saunter in
    without choice, seemingly unbidden. I ask who? They say kin
        but still I wonder who is that listening to my unspoken grin
Look again, a single solitary scientific reservation; more exceptions -
- **MAYBE**

campus of consensually validated facts, an intellectuals' a world-fair
    within ivy towers - white coats seek without preconceived care
        Beakers bubble. Correlations calculate. Science blares!
"Yesterday's magic morphs — revealing today's scientific specs."
    Yesterday – Incomprehensible – now comprehensible by techs
        Look! This moment see myriads of new thoughts intersect
Yet Homo sapiens – are something more than mere matter flecks —
MAYBE

For my ear to hear (incomprehensible magic to the savage unaware)
    White coated geeks reify & measure tiny compressions of air
        Translate: invisible impressions - visible waves that jab.
A baffling mystery: Human hearing revealed in the empirical lab,
    like *floating feathers* (precise impulses) measureable breeze.
        A billion synapses zing and zap - dense feathers seize.
Invisible exceptions: dog whistles please & whale sounds tease. –
MAYBE

Lens Eyes (*believers* defend human eye God's unique holy gift)
    Vast photons undulating waves or discrete particles and shift
        as science scans, godless sophisticates peek, and name
lens, retinas, optics, not God eye — occipital brain sees & exclaims:
    No myths or unfathomable mystically magic — just actual fact.
        Not eye-lens - sight is by a billion bead occipital abacus.
Among the exceptions are infrared and ultraviolet feedback. –
MAYBE

MRI Cortex — lift a car hood - motor running - behold sans hesitation:
    Billions of Synapses - cerebral voices embracing resonation.
        Consciousness, woo woo god, is in the lab today revealed
Diced, sliced, probed, measured, examined poked and peeled
    Independent variables not variable or independent. Defer myths
        A hundred trillion She/He/It gods breathe free forthwith
Proviso: to let Santa Claus be done, and ancient magic monoliths. –
MAYBE

New Scientific Facts — garnered like a herd of cats into a stainless steel sacks.
    For *the faithful - continued existence believing is comfort and survival* even though it lacks evidence or accumulated data of point-at-able natural facts—
DEFINITELY

One of the major debates being ironed out in the halls of science—both physical and sociological—is the concept of 'morality' and its application to current law reform.

If a myriad of neural, genetic and environmental variables, rather than human "free will" is the prime cause of behavior, where do we place responsibility?

What will replace the totally unreliable twelve-peer panel on future juries?

MORAL TERROR

In place of the distressingly unresponsive
   celestial idol or foxhole god
believing fundamentalists insinuate, pissed off Father/god with rod
to punish & then hide at natures brink. Seems of Him strange to tell
His ideal creation of the tormenting, fires of Gehenna, Hades & Hell

Contrast today's science frees a savage" mind from hell-fire tripe
   & finds moral terror of torture unnecessary - to be a decent type.
     Sciences spots ethical action in nature and gracious possibilities
humans honor paradoxical life and continuous potentialities

Trusty fundamentalists lay canards damning evolution's eloquence
"without eternal hell belief or antithetical correlated coincidence
   Homo sapiens possess blood red tooth & claw villain birthrights."
Science says "we are biological creatures climbing new heights."

Paradoxical we are: conflict-cooperation killing- kindly yang and yin
   More to do with where than with nether-land threats labeled sin
     We're not the only moral critter: dolphins behave empathetically
Naturalism spins a web of enchantment and fructifying spirituality

We mammals evolved to cherish & sacrifice for clans common good.
   Innate propensities conflict & aggression fade, as hatred would
Not because a grand skyhook plucked us from a fabled garden edict
But because evolved consciousness demands of us: Reflect!
Perceive! Predict!

The popular counsel to be "passionate," to "love unconditionally" and to "just accept people as the are" is revisited in the following somewhat tongue in cheek poem.
We are asked to look again at these fashionable life-style bits of advice. And once again, question the authenticity of the accepted wisdom.

THINKING ABOUT THE PASSIONATE LIFE?

Passion: Think about it! Can't? Then seek Webster:
Dictionary defines Passion: Agony, Pain or Suffering.
The "Passion Play": a sand box of crisscross slides:
A pain-full, woeful howl of Christ's double-cross cry

Think about it! Seek it! Evangelicals bawl:
Pursue life with passion. I linger, I ponder:
Oh agreed! Right, almost every<u>thing</u>
I pursue - becomes an ass aching fall

Think about it! From self-proclaimed gurus
The Words: "accept with unconditional love".
Momentarily blank. What the hell is that?
Who's he talking to – about - or over?

Even babies are required to pee in diapers
Unconditional? Drivel - morphing to gibberish!
Unconditional anything is perjury - a fantastic fantasy
I have - you have - we all have conditions!
Think about it!

How about this:
"I accept - just the way you are!"
Are you kidding? More BS - eventually twaddle!
When my dank dirty dark shows (or yours!)
The absurd declaration is seen for what it is.
Think about it!

We demand others be reasonable,
We believe that molesters change
Such "reasonable" expectations eventually
divulge more morphed passionate pain
Think about it!

Thinking about the passionate life?
Think again!

Here's another of what some have called a cynical noir monochrome poem. Popular media, if it wants to stay in business, must present a biased view that will appeal to the large demographic of patriotic citizens.
Sometimes it can be disconcerting (or refreshing) to see another point of view.
Or maybe not?

I knew the origin of war was in each of us. I knew that our concept of the hero was outdated,
that the modern hero was the one who would master his own neurosis so that it would not become universal, who would struggle with his myths, who would know that he himself created them, who would enter the labyrinth and fight the monsters. The wars we carried within us were projected outside.
— Anais Nin

ALICE REMEMBERS HEROES

<u>NY times:</u> "OBL most wanted criminal" Planned 9-11 say sources
Luxuriating in Pakistan? Executed by clandestine special-forces
Yet: Yankee millions flowed to Osama named by Alice. Confusion?
Hero mirror — pipeline-defender stopped Russian Afghan intrusion
<u>Remember</u>? Go Ask Alice about heroes

Washington Post - Saddam Husain cruel Iraqi dictator with WMDs.
Labeled: "terrorist & tyrant" given "fair trial"& hanged in the breeze.
Early on - Alice's sees Husain as 'Freedom Fighter' for Iraqi soil
Given arms & Yankee payment - resist Iranian incursions to Iraqi oil
<u>Who remembers</u>? Go Ask Alice about heroes

New York Times: Kaddafi bombed (not killed) by American will
"crimes against humanity" allowed Libyan mob liberators to kill
Yet: Kaddafi looked into the magical history glass - an ally ongoing
America's kind friend and assistant while the Libyan oil was flowing —
<u>You Remember</u>? Go ASK Alice about heroes.

Washington politicians - elevated clerics - boast of heroes gamely
Safely ensconced, promote maimed teen-age heroes & death mainly
Although it's been said *"unhappy is the land that breeds no heroes"*
No! says rebel Galileo *"unhappy is the land that needs heroes*!!"
<u>We remember now</u>! ASK Alice for truth about heroes:

Moral: lying politicians, party lines, pseudo friendships & oil do insist
Around bleeding globe, America's youthful heroes trendy as syphilis
Look today into Alice's magic mirror at your maimed teen-age hero
Read between blare of headlines – emphasize the question below
Dare any patriot: "<u>remember what the dormouse said</u>?"
ASK ALICE & *feed your head*!!

Numinous Mirrors ♦ 33

During one of my Big Sur Esalen summer poetry classes, one of the published, well-known poets suggested that abstractions were not grist for the poet's mill.

I'm still unclear about the concept. The following poem is an attempt to challenge that assumption in the context of word and mind evolution.

POETIC ANATHEMA

Abstractions: Reality, Truth, Wisdom — Acumen words tangibly wrought.
Said my teacher an adamant bard: "Out damn obtuse speech spots!
Return to your intangible Greek and Latin peripatetic academic sots
We modern composers neither need nor desire debatable uncertainty.
We new progressive poetic word-smithies eschew abstract ambiguity."

Except, this MONTH prevailing brain business steers diverse enigmas to light.
Cleaning and clearing old cerebral riddles, new words spark like fire bright,
"Erase any abstract force," my poet teacher said, "vacate flames from sight."
Still they fly free from word smithies anvil—rise, expand, explode, clone.
Today, contemporaries ask, "What is rite? What is marrow? What is bone?

This WEEK new brain business is about words that fan, flirt and mate
Now reified — abstract *consciousness* can no longer encapsulate.
The *mind ghost* is now visible, concrete to touch, to see, to manipulate
as any other test tube jot, iota or fragmented molecule from A to Z.
We now measure, we now weigh, we now, as never before, do see.

Poet brains, like scientist brains, mostly on autopilot – mine too!
Relish fatty foods; enjoy dilated eyes, seek sleep's slumbered glue
Without choice! Poets bid & woo envious green monsters on cue,
They have little choice over vast machinery running below purview
Consciousness: Once lofty abstraction, now junior board member too,

Poet's foot arrives at car break before once holy *consciousness* – so fair
Poets yawn, think and process darting dog with mille-seconds to spare
Poet's gut, not logic, speaks - unplanned decisions spring from mind's lair.
Poet's mysteriously complex but comprehensible brain neural systems
now (carved by natural and abstract selections) seek survival solutions.

Abstractions, concepts, skillfully facilitate tangible brain-neural expansion
Ancient ancestors, evolved verbs, nouns and invented word augmentation
surely as primordial poet's survival wrought muscle spleen and bowel
TODAY some eager rhymester-poets relish nascent words and scowl
Abstractions no longer anathema! Let the *rutted finicky versifiers* how!

And then, why not all words? Are they not all semiotic?

"The unexamined life is not worth living." The record of Socrates' heresy trial included this statement.

Socrates encouraged his students to question the accepted beliefs of the time and to think for themselves.

For this sentiment he was sentenced to death. Perchance his sentiment is worth a few moments of re-apprising?

DEFINE ME: SKEPTIC OR CYNICAL REALIST

Realist (not cynic, not snob) may define me!
At least how I want to define me, wait and see
Perhaps to some friends I am not pleasing
What do they say? "Surely, he's just teasing".

We all know pseudo intellectuals constant redesigning
Without vaguest understanding of Einstein's saying
("Most incomprehensible thing: it is all comprehensible")
Maybe for you - a true fable. Not me — intellect's unstable

What about human nature? My 'not-cynic' query,
Why do we insist to make it such a weary mystery?
Said PT Barnum: "Insert dime for satisfying story!"
Disregard that nether-land mystical fleckless theory

Readily admitted … Well, mostly just an easy lob.
Labeled a snobby bigot. But Einstein was called snob
by Nazis — Never a racial bigot! So they say.
(Good company to find myself - even half way)

Smiling, Laughing, ridiculing? Who's to blame?
Seems the more outrageous fables they claim
The more worshippers pop out – pay their dimes
And sing relentless praise to silly fairy rhymes.

You feel another rant: Boring shit? Renditions!
Say something about the human condition
not so cynical. Where to find it? Not from kin,
not philosophy, not psychology, not Esalen.

Nostrum declarations bawl and clatter profundity
until one requests another reified, point-at-able ditty
"Extraordinary claims require extraordinary proof".
Said Sagan. So, Naturalistic realists remain aloof

Continuing with the theme of self-examination – poetic discoveries continue: I only abhor in others what I find unacceptable in myself. I do not dislike obesity, I detest intensely the lack of discipline it represents. My lack of discipline is abhorrent to me.

I ABHOR

I admit. I'm a bigot; I abhor a multitude of human qualities
I loathe lax lazy lollygagging & reified philosophies
I avoid dense loafers & dull abstraction and clichés

I abhor corpulent calorie gobblers grumbling - look see!
"The culprit: my gene driven metabolism — not me!"
(by habit's gluttony, reason is beaten to insensibility)

I'm repulsed by stupidity, ignorance & thought atrophy
The presence thereof undoubtedly bliss & for some glee
I abhor each one of these attributes residing - Yes. Within me!

OK! Rightfully, a child fears the label 'outsider' 'new kid', no rapport
Look again 'insider' and 'clique kid' your dreams, are distant vectors
and imaginings collapsed — you hug presumptions of a detached sector

Wise ones still say: "there but for the grace of god-life — I sit!"
Deny? Not me. Avoid? Not I. Embrace? Yes, yes, I do - damn it!!
Who but an apathetic realized fool would, could do this bit?

Can I now confess my own slothful, lazy, indolent witless clown?
When my self-righteous fibrous being shouts: "never be found"
"Inconsistency" my nemesis! – Yet, within my own depth it sounds.

ME! A "nodulized" lens by which my brain shapes my world, my reality
Inevitably, I change — why so difficult? I pretend to be ever so witty
Change the lens thus change me from vaguely adrift to happy giddy

Invulnerable me. Isolated I enter the conflagration - I fight - I give
I am vulnerable and feel the pain of loss and loneliness as elective
I see the moon – I feel small – My problem? Mere perspective!

My month at ESALEN INSTITUTE in Big Sur California afforded an opportunity to explore many and varied perspectives.
During one of the Poetry seminars it was suggested that there is a real danger in accommodating to crowded cities and urban life and thereby mislay the deft hand of quiet nature.
In less than a month "addiction" to Big Sur and its peaceful quiet set in.
Yes, I was addicted to Big Sur's quietude.

ESALEN MYTHS & THE REAL DANGER?

(Each Seminar morning I slog upward to the assembly)
Aching calves sacrificed on Sisyphus's steep sinuous hill
Without stone, in silence I suffer, pleading lungs wilting still
Not alone, I gasp my complaints: Esalen cruelty unfolds
Inflict thy slings and arrows! Outrageous fortunes untold!
my trudges gash me to Poet's Yurt or to Fritz's nest on high
Dangerous? Dangerous? We only guess and sigh. Why? Why?
Olympus Gods know - really know - besides dalliance
dangers not in the climb? Is there danger in silence?

(Each morning I hear words of warning) vis-à-vis a poetic lore
I take today a distinctive path to the summit of truth's whore
danger's in accommodating. Habituating to Sisyphean chores
My bulked-calves, fresh clean air, my sterile spotless pores
My wax-less ears, hot water washed in the magic cliff poured I plead
for another Esalen drug: A steep silent Sisyphean hill
whistle-clean addiction breach insipid sedentary wills shout danger,
danger, and drugged true-life danger again - again
leisurely strolls into hard-core silence now my addictive friends
Big Sur's sweet dangerous silence now my new addiction.
Dare I return to city domain with this new-heart-felt restriction?

In the Esalen writing class we were asked to write a short paragraph about the reasons for failed love. Blocked for what are now to me obvious reasons, I wrote a very brief paragraph, which when read out loud, I stumbled and stammered so that the time allotted passed and I sat down without bringing it to an end. Later I attempted to finish it with the following result:

INTENTIONS

She was (I thought) my best Pygmalion creation,
Still, on some veiled level I must have known (I knew):
Her self-made image was only temporarily subdued
in the bubbling spring of rainbow and unicorn love
she knew me, not only as Eve knew Adam,
she knew, I contend, the glistening purity of my heart.
In bed between snowy sheets no secrets were held,
shared intimacies; cherished fantasies of other loves.
"Warts and all." Said to remind one another of our immunity
There were no warts of course but we both knew flaws
I thought, I believed, I considered that we loved them all.

The truth, a truth, my truth, ill timed I reiterate & blurt to her
It stung! I blithely smiled and giggled, like a hebephrenic nut.
Other words would have given thanks or apology - left unsaid
(as if they were mere minor unnecessary social conventions,
superfluous in our mutually created totally lucid/opaque world).
My lumbering number 12s crushed our un-bloomed blossoms
along with promises and her single susceptible sentient heart.
How could this be? I feigned, "It's unclear to me- I'm so confused!"
My cloudy claim: "I am untainted positively pure of heart"
I used many tissues and a few glands for tears
but produced silly laughter along side the sobs

E-mails, later revealed weepy missives of need
and were seen by my naive tear glazed eyes
as more cosmic jokes. More contrived laughter.
From simulated 'out blue' a sudden single reveal.
I was/am branded - the scarlet letter A. - for asshole.
"Words", I pontificated in rebuttal, "are but puffs of air.
Compressed and sent to a brain for interpretation:
You see me as EVIL but spell it backwards." I grinned.
Never lacking for repartee retorts, I blundered on
digging deeper my well-intentioned - splintered casket
The single Word Goodbye, I discovered, not just a puff of compressed air
It hurt ... and hurts still

Occasionally, word definitions have need of elucidation: And even then—tell half-truths—because, as one of my wisdom-filled friends once said, "Words can't help but lie."

TALENT AND GENIUS

Talent sees, improves upon and actualizes what is already here
Genius sees what is not here — nudges and imbues it without fear

Talent allows for crazy pop trends to morph and advance
Genius revolutionizes the popular trends sans olive branch

Talent balks, and makes trouble for the ordinary
Genius mutates and makes fresh the extraordinary

Talent views the field and decides what to do next
Genius ignores the field - decides what NOT to do next

Talent nuances and modifies the varieties and tastes of chewing gum
Genius accepts "we judge covers" that tell us where tastes come from

Talent will assess the risk and defy the odds and accepts failure and quits it
Genius intuits the odds, takes creative risks; defies failure, and just DOES IT

Talent is able to achieve a goal no one else can reach
Genius is able to attain a goal no one else can distinguish

Talent sings on key and inspires the choir with lofty words: Carpe Diem
Genius marches to another beat and *Carpes* the hell out of Diem

Talent ever seeks a solution and cries love, caring and other similitude
Genus knows life is apparent within the roil of forgiveness and gratitude

Early on, I wondered about the essence of life and the oft-mentioned "afterlife."
In what state does one leave this world? Then I heard: "How does wetness leave water?"
Maybe its not totally hard science but it made sense to me.

WAVE FABLE

Really ... look and see:
There is a little wave, bobbing along in the ocean,
It's having a wonder-filled time.
He/she/it is enjoying the wind
as well as its own wetness and the fresh air!
Until it stops and then notices
other waves bobbing
crashing against the shore.

"My God, this is horrible!" the little wave says,
"Look what's going to happen to me!"
Then along comes another wave.
It sees the first wave, looking grim,
"Why do you look so sad? It asks.
The first wave quivers and quavers
"You don't understand! We're all going to crash!
All of us waves are smashing and crashing!
It's ghastly appalling and ... ?"

The second little wave replies,
"No, <u>you</u> don't understand
REALLY... LOOK AND SEE
You're not only a wave,
You are the ocean."
Nothing is lost in
this Universe

In the early 60s I heard the Zen philosopher Alan Watts utter: "As the ocean waves - God peoples"
As the years passed that utterance made even more sense to me.
I trust the following makes sense to you.

THE OCEAN METAPHOR

Metaphors bring magic and meaning:
       As the Ocean Waves ... so GOD Peoples.
    As oft as I can,
   I seek the Pacific shore
  watch unremitting ocean *waves*
 incessantly pop from their prodigious,
powerful and persuasive wet marine matrix.
I allow my speculative imagination to witness wetness
the myriads multitude of rising escalating singular *waves*:
"*People*" rising, multiplying, egotistically shouting, "*I am - I am
I AM so important and so very significant that unquestionably
there is a supernatural everlasting future set aside just for me!
(Mansions, streets of gold, lush gardens or 72 nymphs) reasonably
MY matrix the eternal ocean selected me TO BE!*" Shout the *waves*
"*Here I am! I am rising up and up and up distinctively and individually.
When I shed this water-wave shell covering
I have unshakeable belief (sometimes
called faith or hope or just belief)
my omnipresent, omniscient,
oceanic creator matrix now
has something really
extraordinary for
"Me."*

Then, the mystical transformation:
watch as *wave* after *wave*
merges with prodigious,
powerful,
    potent marine matrix.
     from which they
      were created.
       Continuously
      Endlessly

In that miraculous zeitgeist merging moment,
they now and forever undoubtedly discern:
WE, you and me, are never apart from the oceanic-creator.
The molecules of multitudinous *waves* "in a twinkling of an eye"
are remixed into googolplex-ian omnipresent, omniscient, ocean matrix.
Will tiny *wave* multitudes (distinctively and individually) come to exist
again?
These Multitudinous *waves* seem perfectly content to be parceled
and merge with their astonishing, prodigious and powerful
ocean matrix. Knowing nothing is ever lost in our
"metaphorical" universe. "In God we *waves*
live and move and flow
back into our being!"
Consciousness
too, is a
meta
phor
...

Then too, Tom Robbins once said, "Human beings are something water invented to get itself carried around."
It seems with water as the metaphor there are always some more words.

H_2O

There is
The mystery
Of water:

In water
We live and move
And have Our being

Water created
Diverse People
To get itself carried
From Diverse Place
To Diverse Place

Clearly
Purely
Plainly
yet
Invisibly

H_2O
Is
The
Daily
Miracle
Of Life

Recently a new clinic opened at Harvard University to scientifically study why Placebos - "the power of nothing," work to heal certain people. So far, there are some people who appear to be more genetically viable to Placebos. Others, without the "gene complex," don't respond well to "suggestions".

PLACEBO – NO-CEBO & CYCLES

Unspoken, but not so delicate Darwinian rivalries spring to life
  Out of own fear of our own insignificance and prideful belief
    A subset of our own childish dread of impending mortality
      We seek accolades rather than authentic achieving

The miracle of human life is much more than molecules
  More than sums of biology and physics' whirling atoms
    Our moral/ ethical verbiage facilitates human wellness
      Our Art, songs and aesthetics heal human illness

"Your ailment - all in your head," says supercilious specialist
  Evil words - heedless of fundamental human life miracles
    Objective data - only half right. *Subjective* speaks the rest
      Quantity/Quality of personal testimonies articulate volumes

The unveiled Genome also testifies - a question few dare to ask
  Do Genes in people who respond readily to placebos - differ?
    Are some wise humans genetically destined not to heal via 'magic'?
      Compelling data suggests answer is: of course, "it looks that way"

Expectations and suggestions - viable for fools who with joy - heal
  Mystical, deceitful influences creep in - what brain expects - affects!
    Neuro-science - measures power of 'nothing' to produce healing
      Prefrontal cortex insists future wellbeing MRIs will witness it

Other outcomes — not objective outcomes — life's ironic outcomes
  Subjective assertions bash & clash scientific methodology proofs
    SEE! The patient says, "I feel better!" biased improvement denied
      gee, patient feels better? Ignore it! *Double-blind numbers don't fib"*

In hale, Ex-hale - day time, night time - eat food, expel waste - perceived cycles
    The rotation beat goes on: the up and down, the in and out, the over and under
    Ill and well, live - die, something – nothing, coming and going- dualities abound
    Zenith of illness – cycles of wellness! Ingested pill is oft a mere bystander

Wellness is as wellness does. So now tell me, does "belief" count for naught?
    But then just how does deceitful, mystical practices creep in so surreptitiously
    How does PT Barnum succeed without believers? He doesn't do very well
    But then, know too that so called double blind studies requires biased observers

Politicians and religionists have long known that just the sheer repetition of a statement will eventually provide perceived veracity. Repeat a "storied myth" until it becomes believable — a new faith will be born.

FREE WILL AND SPIRITUALITY

Ancient entertaining fables are but truth-full works of fiction
Causal reality shows them premised by ongoing neural invention
Thus immediate media, repetitive thought, synaptic cyclic replication
Impact - placate - modify - pacify - calcify - mollify by mere reiteration

Demonstrated by recent neuro-science (fMRI & SPECT scan)
socio-religious values - whimsically shaped via *stuff* than can
be peddled from pulpits, high definition screens, reality scams
and multi-colored-pseudo-news tabloids that imitate I Pad loads

Underlying contention? Just the mere recurrence of *stuff*
(*uber-beliefs, myths, magic, hyped metaphorical pious fluff*)
Provides believability in chronic patterns & redundant information,
repeated fables and foibles truly change human brain formation

Thus your perception of today's reality - by just such repetition
is modified – top-end human brain nodules morph transformation.
Repeat "Hail Mary" - "Allah is great", new brain assemblies are spun
Now thus infected, our futile seeking of *free will hype* becomes a dry run

Assume if you wish, but your *free will* is a myth, like other Eden's
Hells and purgatories, invented to frighten evil and govern good men
One moment HE loves, the next HE invidiously exacts. Some now laud
fear, retribution and punishment eternally done by some angry jealous god

Why your obsequious believing when thinking provides renaissance?
There's the rub! Belief rides on simple blind deference and easy adherence
Skeptical thinking needs continual questioning, requiring seeking, critiquing
Within curiosity (not acquiescence) discover awe, wonder & spiritual speaking

Think of how often familiar old sayings, are repeated as truth. And how often we take them at face value. And how often we refuse to offer a resounding – BUT!

WRONGLY THEY SAY:

They say,
"Experience is the best teacher"
    I say marvelous *mind's* magical "memory" is greater
I make an intact future by my experience, & I provide the teacher

They say,
"Beauty' is in the eyes of the beholder"... beauty renewal?
    I say seduction is the champion - Evolution's tool — human survival
We protect, shelter even serve what seduces love's revival

They say,
"It's a man's world" yes, what's left? A wounded, dying mess
    I offer condolences and sadness. To "his" grandchildren "he" doesn't confess
Only women seem to possess care genes to save, nurture and bless

They say,
"Don't count your chicks." Polygamy - another of man's handiworks
    He counts scalps - brags to panting insufficient males who anxiously lurk
What do chicks have to do with the cause of arrogant male quirks?

They say,
"It's darkest before dawn" Paradox: Wrong becomes right
    I suggest dark matter matters in such we work, play - have sight
Dark matter erupts & vacates space for the ambient warmth of light

They say,
"Honey badgers don't give a shit!" Because they can't
    I insist: An outsized body and earless head can only rant
Stuck in evolutions survival by rage and hate. Brainless as an ant

They say,
"A child should be seen — not heard." Why be a child?
    I suggest a higher purpose. Children are created not to be mild
But to show lame illiterate ones the beguile of a reserved wild child

They say
"God was a man" or at the very least a prophet of doom
    I assert death is no surprise to followers who shout too soon
But if come the resurrection believers have the laughable tune

They say
"Live in the moment" but the HERE & NOW is now passed and so
    Even the sun that warms your hottest passion lived eight minutes ago
"Living the moment" as the tune above: Factually supplementary hot blow

Seems every poet I know, must write about poetry at one time or another. This may not be science only because I have not sufficiently studied human "obsessions" deeply enough.

POETRY

I wish I could write living poetry with fire and desire
Yet disbelief burns upon my *mind's* unquenchable pyre
Scarring and burning deep my naive unmarred soft sheath
Some Words live and sear again, my calloused underneath

Poems evolve in my *mind's* labyrinthine of some known truth
And breathe understanding to expunge a few ideas - uncouth
So if I allow the suffering sights and sounds of fire's poetic pain
To come forth in nascent newness nevermore to fade or wane

Then out! And on to the dark mystery! I incessantly descend
never wanting, yet still beholding faith's complete story's end
My droll desperate poetry still tells tales of disloyal denouement.
Fact be told, bona fide sage sayings are dipped from excrement

Inspired stories: *'comas'*, release us from the eternal human drama
Denounce faith, hope and belief and all that is said by a Dalai Lama
Mere subset of our eternal dread of obvious mortality yet still promised
"We arrogant mortals have to be immortal," assure the poetic Palmists

The poets may pledge to cease carving poetry for such transport
Because they oft demure - poems tell lies - language distorts
But what can we say that gets it right even that modest much?
Our myths pervert but poems perhaps, our hearts may touch

*A FUN EMAIL was received during the summer 2012. The Author or concept was and is still unknown to me
Because of the following, perhaps it should stay that way!*

6
WHERE I LIKE TO GO. OR NOT!

I've been in many places, but I've rarely been in Cahoots
these days. Apparently, you can't go alone and to boot.
You have to be in Cahoots with someone en route.

I sometimes play-act In-cognito.
Pretend no one - not friend or foe
recognizes the real me-schmo .
I like that - except for the undertow.

I have often been in Sane.
No road map or marked lane,
I've driven there by missionary kind
I have been in the double bind,
Thanks to the wheels of my own mind.

I would like to go to Conclusions, but I have to jump,
and I'm not too much on activity – I'm such a lazy lump.

I have also been in Doubt. That's a wondrous place to go,
I visit there oft as I can. Keeps me curious and in the know

I've been in Flexible, too often. Excused by saying
"But, but, it was only *principle* I was stoutly relaying".

Sometimes I'm in Capable, and I go there more often than I should
Especially now I'm getting older, and entering my second childhood.

One of my favorite places to be is in Suspense!
It gets my adrenalin flowing yet makes no sense
pumps up the old heart! And flushes my sagging skin!
At my age I need some discipline or maybe the loony bin

Sometimes the truth about oneself is hard to swallow. At some other times a necessity because sometimes even a cathartic can be a positive healing experience.

THE SOMETIME PERIL OF RISK

I am old - decades of gray
   If I can speak honestly each day
      In obdurate times I would have to say:
         "I know nothing!" – Most times...

Sometimes I've leapt into life's sea with joy.
   Altogether missing love's celebrated life Buoy.
      To searing pain and detriment sometimes
         To wonder - awe - and surprise most times.

I am old and I say: Listen! –
   There is magic in each day.
      A life without surprise - a cage
         Life without churning - too beige

I am old and I say: Yes! Sometimes
   I have glimpsed vulnerability's wake
      Sometimes times are painful and bleeding
         Throbbing dramatically yet real ne'er fake

So, sometimes when I really take note
   I say stop - declare your costly blunder
      Release the humdrum of a negative vote
         Choose the whirling watery jumble of wonder

Yes, I'm old & I say: Stop repeating the vain prance
   Now and again - feel the wash and peril of Titanic
      And the sense defenselessness acutely enhanced
         by an exhilarated blunder to the edge of icy/fiery panic

Where now besides the nausea roil of sea sick's flu?
   Or the other: The astonishing dream comes true!
      Sometimes the dread ends with a dicey misconstrue:
         Of her sometimes ambiguous wooly words "I love you!"

As a child I loved magic and fairy-tale answers — Actually magic is required material for exceptional childhood development.
Adults continuing fairy tale solutions are denying maturity and its accompanying "shadow dance".
Accepting the "shadow" is also reality as surely as inhaling is reliant on exhaling — Both are part and parcel of wisdom. Both are reality.

A SATISFYING DANCE WITH A SHADOW

I am oft forced by my rants too long
To seek my progenies' sublime song:
Dance with the Shadow ... Dad
"Dancing, embracing, accepting — not bad."
But veering off to some make-believe fantasy
Leaves only a vacuum waste, instead of me
not a satisfying answer for me to see.

When we solo dance, my sweet, sweet dear
we keep the beat, partnering a mirror.
Together, we savor inhaling and opposite, the exhaling
forward and converse, backwards reeling
the up-beat and contrary, downbeat feeling.
Beyond doubt, such a dance is living in the oneness of now.
Some pretend a oneness of physics and metaphysics somehow
math & numerology, astronomy & astrology's moon-cow,
not satisfying answers in this our adult modern now.

Wed nature to super nature – upshot: bewildered meanings.
like saying December 25 (a date) & Santa Claus (inventing-s)
are one and forever the believable same thing.
Like saying 4:20 is clock time — wow! ding ding
Like a wedding of chemistry to mythical alchemy
Even medieval Merlin understood that's no key
Not real satisfying answers for you or for me.

There're some (mostly women - who please)
sensitive to life's many unseen subtleties,
& realities existing as virulent similitude.
They're sensitive & deny their own aptitudes
instead attribute their endowments to fantasies
and myths osmosis-ed as kids — to please
gurus who exchange *knowledge* for fees
claimed from some other dimension - they profit
(for one thin time they will teach the "secret")
Not satisfying answers for this miscreant.

Following WWII Piper Aircraft produced thousands of small canvas covered aircraft. They were little yellow tandem seated airplanes. They could practically fly themselves. At least that is what my Instructor often said. In those days they were the airplanes of choice for beginners learning to fly. I was one of them.

ANTIGRAVITY — A YELLOW PIPER CUB

A little yellow cub taught me to fly
I learned to glance and watch up high
and down for haven, like a hungry waif
for my mâché paper *Piper* to land me safe

But I also learned how mist and clouds must feel
And touched the cold of azure blue and felt it yield
We did fly up so high, felt sky's unfeigned freedom
Discovered the real true meaning "thy Kingdom come"

I can smile and laugh at earthbound god-things
Because now I know the real reason birds sing
I continually heard their harmonic song on high
And my society's laughable meaning of goodbye

I learned to soar and defy gravities' tug
So that now in these golden years I'm smug,
content, sometimes daftly happy, because I sought
not a mythical god, but a yellow cub — as my copilot

I learned, not just once but seemingly repetitively
the so-called mysterious meaning of life's relatively
Today I envy no earthbound mortals or gods on high
Because a modest, little yellow cub taught me to fly

The science of computerized Matchmaking is well documented.
But even without external computers there is evidence that we have
a kind of "Match-making app" available when we need it in the
eternal search for
the other.

SAY YES TO BLIND DATING

After a mutual matchmaker *Yentle*
bawled at me: "stop being so mental
just act!" Say yes! I said yes, yes.
We met in a bar a Juice bar—I'd guessed
Eyes flashed as invectives non-blessed!

Yes—I'm failing to make the grade — meaning
  Yes, I'm called - an un-evolved spiritual being.
    Yes, I am skeptical not Pollyannaish leaning
      Yes, I am questioning not blindly consenting,
        Yes, sometimes I am just life's plaything
          Yes, life's natural end is death's final name
            Yes, paradise to come is a con man's refrain

No doubt I'd try but I'm doomed as such
Her fevered fervent judgment said as much
So how do I stop the lament? - And find that "other"
The one able and rather willing to move thru further
past mythologies and comforting mythical murmurs
without appeal to tales of space-men voyageurs?

Kurzban's University research reveals,
   That regardless of what "single people" *conceal*,
     That they need only seconds with the potential
      That yes, is real; they're attending with zeal.
       That behavior suggests they know the rite
        That the person who appeals sees "it"
         That immediately "it" feels and <u>is</u> real.

Yes! Pennsylvania research studied mate & date.
Men and women assessed in seconds compatibilities' fate
visual cues: age, height, color and attractiveness do rate.
Fits with my first criterion please, tease and she'll
release Dopamine via "grooming and sex appeal"
research says, "some factors you might think real
like religion, education, and income" — don't reveal.

In my recent experience — I was judged and vetted
   I didn't explore income — or from whence she Lear Jetted
     I discover her education in a fundamentalist muddy bog
       Is anathema to meaningful or any open non-scripted dialog?
        I know I am choosy; particular biased and lack a heartthrob
         I am skeptical but curmudgeons are people too – I feel robbed
          I am grateful, energetic and curious about other thingamabobs

Even with love, we sometimes forget that all of us are here for the time being, intrinsically vulnerable to the passage of time, old age, illness and death. This is our common fate and nothing, but our own personal fantasies, psychoses' and denials will keep us from the confrontation of this reality.

As pessimistic as this may sound to some, no matter how talented we are, or gifted, no matter how many stocks or yachts we own, we are all exquisitely, excruciatingly exposed to the fact that soon than later our place at the table will be cleared and we will be gone. The mind games we play, to expunge this fact is why anti-science is so vital to religionists of all sorts.

But more often than not, in the presence of love, something softens within us, our hurry slows and worries seem to mollify to acceptability. For most committed scientists, nothing survives death unless it continues on in this living. Immediate living in the here and now can and does allow motivation to seek and find the other. For in that synergistic moment, eternity is beheld in mirrored certitude.

WHAT'S THE POINT WITHOUT LOVE?
?
No
Nay nix
Old words to
Say what is less?
Answers a double yes
You have truth from above
The fact - I'm not easy to love!
Skeptics are never easy to love but
Determined love can be a careless rut
Skeptics know life 'with' and 'without' love
The worth of 'with' is adoring and being adored
'Without' is lightless, dull and the feeling of bored
Sometimes 'with' feels like an unbelievable paradise
While 'without' is motionless, sightless, lifeless compromise
'With' means danger from the churn and swirl of blunt decisions
'Without', has no such endorphin drug-laden motivating inspirations
'With', a heart may daily sing boisterous melodious songs of gratitude
'Without' feels deserted, and now devoid of the *other's* mirrored certitude
'With" is to see it all again for the first time each day celebrating rectitude
I'm a skeptic. I love the 'with' but "I'm not easy to love" it's my ineptitude
'Without" may motivate, & sweep one downward and away from sight
'With' makes the summer last and with a single kiss defines delight
'Without' isolates while "with" a single night may end the plight
Sometimes 'with' can feel akin to a plunge through thin ice
'Without' I become frozen stiff akin to a taut dildo device
Sometimes 'with' senses the holy plausible paradise
'Without' can also create its' own mind attraction
'With' often brings body and soul satisfaction
Skeptics are never easy or ready to love
Then why care if I fit the social glove
I always say yes to every invite
Knowing how to really delight
Actually we all do know
the resolution to all—
simply answer
love's call
say yes

Most of the time
Metaphysics is a substitute for real fulfillment.
It is a mind game we play with physics.
By adding a "meta" we can creep up alongside physics and pretend
we have something to hold on to...
at least in a "meta" sense.

METAPHYSICS & MYSTICISM

What is God?
Or... Where is God hiding?
The Clinical Psychology specialists at USC
Were not prone to answer such questions
The answer: "there is no answer!"
Or how would you know what is unknowable?
Such answers did not compute at University
Where in that time, behaviorism was god.

Where is God today?
The answer is un-reachable – un teach able
Or paradoxically that which is unknowable
Can with discipline and solitude be knowable
The solitary monk seeks God in isolation
And solitude, prayer, meditation, auto hypnosis
Rhythmic mantras, mind pulse and heart beat as one

What is God?
Where is God found?
In meditation the lone mystic hears
Sweet rapturous melodies & sees visions
Within and without his heart heated breast
uber-active imagination & fervid delusion mix
Madness and the unreeling of endless mind tapes
Empirical *'sensory deprivation'* experiments duplicate

What is God?
Where is God home?
Mystics claim God is the life cradle endlessly rocking
In salacious mind storms calmed by nonstop mantras
Such mysticism is appealing for some - perhaps most
Empiricism will not claim it! Something is missing
in this living within, ravished by things unseen,
lean-ness of longing now gone. Desire-less-ness prevails
madness or saint-ness induced by deprivation and mortification?

What is God?
Where is God?
Am I able to live within the cloud of eternal unknowing?
I am curious; I see science as immediate but temporary knowing
Then the next exciting question peaks & my curiosity tears off
Through mystery corridors and experimental design's correlations
To empirical repeatable testable consensually validated revelations
Where the things unseen are revealed in the aperture of things seen
I listen to the song in the wind but I anchor in the rock of science

In ancient Greece marble statuary was famous for its aesthetic and near perfect pure white marble forms. When Rome took over "LAW" was enshrined in place of aesthetics. The result: Roman marble artisans made marble statues filled flaws and then filled the flaws with beeswax and sold them as "perfect" to unsuspecting customers. As a result the Romans were said (albeit incorrectly) to have enacted another LAW: To sell a marble statue as perfect it must be stamped — SIN (without) CERA (wax)

Thus: If you are sincere — you are without wax!!

(Allegedly an old wives tale, the fanciful inaccurate history is still worthy of a poem.)

SINCERE

For Greek advocates
Aesthetics did dominate
from vast marble excavation
pure white slabs scored and spun
Conveyed to light and tooled 'till done
Carved, chiseled, polished, elegant erection
Aesthetic angels emerge in flawless perfection

In ancient Rome
Law fixed by chromosome
Took those same marble slabs, hone
from enormous blocks of precious stone
filled flaws with beeswax and then bemoaned
the new full-blown LAW: wax cannot be condoned
Sin Cerea- without wax- is now the latest law of Rome

Often for me, the best answer I can often offer is: "I don't know." And to learned professors I have been heard to say "And frankly, I don't really think you do either!"

WHAT I DON'T KNOW
the meaning of
LOVE. (Definitions)
How to live out loud that puzzling word?
  Verb, noun, adjective, adverb - absurd
    seize squeeze & find spoilt lemon curd
      new connotations born each new hour
        of each new day to amaze - and flower
LOVE. (Tangles)
Love conundrums, labyrinths to daze & amaze!
The fecund twisted conduit - love is indeed a maze.
  providing the bent puzzling channeled craze
    grabbed by hot contemporary U Tube talkers
      or chic interludes by kitschy life coach mockers
LOVE (Morphs)
I love her. I love oranges — I seize the lingering mood
  Ever seeking yet trapped by ever squeezing ineptitude.
    Sequester zest? If only I could fix forever a love attitude
      Is it Gourmet nourishing cuisine or expeditious fast food?
        Know love? I know the gracious feeling of gratitude

the latest definitions of
SPIRITUALITY (Airy)
I don't know how to define this other plum
  an ethereal whatever — called by some
    "spirituality". Do you believe *thy kingdom come?*
      or doubt the hum drum and then run far from
        spirit rum? holy spirit glum? school spirit fun?
SPIRIT (A Show)
Reify: a word meaning to make an abstract something
  Into a some-thing concrete with an earthy solid ring
    Spirit – pneumatic – wind – vaporous hot air malign
      Materialize IT for the needful youthful child minds
        make abstract concrete with a visible shine
SPIRIT (trade name)
Indeed, I suppose children need to reify— true!
  if you too must make some-thing out of the blue
    make solid the abstract no-thing work for me <u>and</u> you
      but to perfect that meme you need an infinite crew
        to bring substance and consensual agreement too

How could any of us know what is unknowable?
OR
How to describe a God for today's world?
The answer is un-reachable – un teach able
Or paradoxically that which is unknowable
Can be knowable.
"The most incomprehensible thing in this
Universe ... is it is all comprehensible."

WHAT I STILL DON'T KNOW

I don't know how to describe

GOD (??)
mad man made god in his image - mad god?
  Then I'll spell it backwards: dam god - dog
    Jehovah, God the Father, Allah — all males
      they've done their best its true, to regale
        the elegant gender to second-class and failed
          Her smart superior wily ways are not for sale

GOD (Omni)
I don't know or wish to know how to be religious
  Especially in the confines of static ritual use
    Please! Get bachelor God married or gone altogether
      then all nature is holy - to infinity - including weather
        I don't know the value of repetition hymns so clever
          But I do know how to be of service & curious forever

GOD (DOG backwards)
I don't know about prophecy's relations
  But I know correlations are not causations
    I taste sunlight - and glimpse the smell of pie
      ethereal feelings to my mind, my tongue and eye
        Odd bone and skin feelings or my memories flung
          to there & here & 'see' only still another song sung

WHAT WE CAN KNOW
But she/we know sweetness in new mown hay
and flirty nature's daze and her infinite holy ways
I do know how amazing wonder becomes unlocked
As when I stride outside my long seized comfort box,
And question, putting prized beliefs aside un-mocked
and quest, garbed in spiritual cloth of curiosity's paradox
I ask - question all, find fresh meanings in Pandora's box

When applying for a particular position I sent in an Email with an electronic signature and my engineer friend suggested that if the Board of Directors desired, they could throw application out and argue that electronic signatures are not valid because it is still a gray area. In fact, he argued that at least 50% of our world is still a gray zone.

A LAWYER'S WORLD OF GRAY QUESTIONS

There is an opaque world
Where lawyers make-believe irate
arguments - filter micro fine points
of law and adversarial debate
In the gray zone

Pakistan physician now guilty of treason
for exposing a vicious 9-11 slayer
And why do politicians perjure and lie
for interminable layer after layer?
In the gray zone

Are computer signatures valid?
Is election fraud always a given?
Do hominids cause global warming?
Is religion relevant or even Zen?
In the gray zone

Should we fight the good fight
in the murky world of opaqueness?
Never achieving or reaching the top
Or not even the bottom muddiness.
In the gray zone

Why not just name religion irrelevant
And move on by - in fervent curiosity
To new wondrous living dimensions
Concepts made on and on incessantly
In a new gray zone

With the advent of new brain scan tools the science of neurology has grown exponentially.
It appears that Science now knows enough to begin asking the appropriate questions.
Even "consciousness" itself is within purview.

BRAIN EVOLUTION

Our brain has evolved just enough
To trick us into believing
We are something more
than mere mechanistic animals.

Your brain fires a million-trillion synapses
And carefully counts genomes
and white cell infections
as we bash and kill each other

World's ruin grinds under our feet
Like bits of sea salt
Crunching and denting
Many a sole - but never our soul.

In the stillness of night if you listen
and hear the tom tom
of heart and pulse
You feel & then see we can be one

Evolution's endless durable patience
What can we learn anew?
From that old brain trick
Aware and announcing we're not that

Then reduce us to rubble! And perhaps
Next time we will learn
From a differently evolved brain
We are loving/lovable & curious animals

One of the great questions: why are we here?
The basic, always avoided, never acknowledged motive:
"To care for 'them' as long as possible."
Are we mere vehicles to carry the micro mega-world from one generation to the next?
Undoubtedly, 'they' will survive even if we do not!

MEGATROPOLIS

Getting them to get along
In faultless synergistic balance
Is that the trick they say it is?
Not that those sticky slimy bugs
like viruses, yeasts and bacteria
that weight in and make up
the major percents of me
will ever be in flawless balance

My body, is actually a super-city
Of super-bugs and microbes and
Living in me an on me like
the count of six and a half billion
persons living on mother Gaia
Not counting atoms, neuro-cells
And molecules by the billions
of bubbling, fizzy chemistry
seeking stasis and splendid balance

If I, not my living thriving others
Living in me, on me , around me
have purpose, what is <u>my</u> teleos?
Then is my life span less counted
Or should we count their life more
when balances proves me healthy
When not, provides me death
Potential health is not me or mine
but my bug-dwelling megatropolis
to determine. I am here to care for them.

One has only to find a light-less wilderness vantage point to vaguely begin to view and comprehend the infinity of mass and energy of our visible cosmos.

Yosemite Valley is such a place.

Is there life out there? I think so, but I don't know for sure — yet.

YOSEMITE NIGHT SKY

Under the night Yosemite sky,
Even before gazing at familiar Dippers,
Heaven's unremitting lights besiege our senses-
Illuminate our eyes from our minor Milky Way
(Barely a middling size galaxy!)
Our elfin Sun is but a nano-dot on one petite spiral arm
(The life sustaining yet frivolous, by contrast,
sun dot-speck will cinder-ize 5 billion years hence)
Our trivial, by comparison, Earth provisioned
by ice-water comets from beyond
And other quantities of iron and mysterious radioactive elements
not understood
Yet…

Yosemite's extraordinary starry heaven
is but a nano-fraction of one mini galaxy
Beyond our scoped-sight there are a 100 billion others
Beyond and within these 100 billion whirling, exploding masses.
Still another 100 billion spiraling stars
twirl and burst away lights' energy
Each one birthing and dying, ripping, accreting
Then blasting and banging again repeatedly, infinitively
To what end?
Senseless nihilism — bleak nothingness – poignant despair OR mystery
not comprehended
Yet…

"The more our universe becomes comprehensible,
the more our experiential universe seems pointless."
Said Nobel expert physicist Weinberg
Yet, who appointed him or us to announce ultimatums?
We may deflect nihilism. And celebrate the incomprehensible!
Knowing as the mystery grows, as the inherent pointlessness
manifests We can swab and soak in endless gratitude
Rejoicing in something rather than nothing
Why life? Why my life?
We know not!
Yet…?

Buddhism is practiced by about 300 million people around the world. The word comes from 'budhi', 'to awaken'. It has its origins about 2,500 years ago when Siddhartha Gotama, known as the Buddha, was himself awakened (enlightened) at the age of 35.

Buddhist path can be summed up as:

to lead a moral life,

to be mindful and aware of thoughts and actions,

to develop wisdom and understanding.

One must wonder about Tibet and why the choosing the next leader appears to be sooooo ???? (Unenlightened?)

BUDDHISM AND OTHER VAGARIES

The motorized mantra goes round
The temple's wheel of peace turns
Unceasingly the mantra twirls
and looms lit, lighting the night
rolled scrolls spin without ceasing
incessantly under an ornate crown
Providing elucidation or — nightmares

Priests proclaim twirling - whirling – spiraling
Primary positive power - yet the grinding & groaning
milling & mincing can also sound sinister and spine chilling
to trainees. Yet — young believing novitiates take the oath –
Fresh from prostrations, 'taught' believers practice empathy for all –
Their purity of purpose palpable, as if by thought alone
the drones will miss their myriads of blameless victims

Then without admonition or caveat
Yet always known, always expected
Not an IF but simply a WHEN
The charismatic Buddhist demigod,
Takes his last breath, Dies, Departs, merges, Passes-over
(The word to use: Follower's choice)
Just believe – Optimistically - Always hope

With vague hints provided by the belated one
A commission sets a search: The Reincarnated heir —
Boy toddlers — never girls, bugs or beasts —
are allured with enticing decoy toys and few 'true' toys
"held in toddler-hood" by the deified departed one.
The unsuspecting tot who holds the "held"
Declared fresh reincarnated winner

Thus the new revitalize man-god is selected.
But why the risk, why the gamble?
If the belated deified demigod dips into omniscience:
(the place and person) – why doesn't he say before
Departing, merging, passing or dying? Just say:
"Reborn Reawakened Reincarnated is 'this' one!"
No decoy boy-toy utilized or needed

'Taught' believers seek a solemn state
detached, non desirous, non-judgmental
Practice allowing their young hearts to crack open
For all - including child molesters, gang-rapists and serial killers –
Ah yes, detach and fill your eyes with tears for scum!
Far easier said than announced done
Notwithstanding — vagaries do exist

Morning exercise in the Palm Springs 84-degree pool water allows for thought exchange, contemplation, and even commitment especially when the sun shines brightly. When there is little winter sun there are fewer snowbirds in the pool

EXISTENTIAL POOL BLATHER

Today, water beneath & around moves to all the right places
Then silence reigns & softer muscles too move in quietness
No fear in offering just a little piece of memory before it erases
Within the pool, tomorrow's spasms turn or tighten or lighten.

This day, this mini-moment, will not repeat or exist again
Even though we like blathering & talking our morning away
Schools of spontaneous thoughts & words swim by and
away in coordinated unison. Maxim: "tomorrow" — who's to say?

Today's now is present. Memories' splashes may revive regrets
Too soon warmer suns & colder recollections call us up and over
to other more extra and ordinary tasks & obligatory mind sets
Culpability's guilty spasms may return & stick like a frosty mantle.

Today we may inhale beauty all around in warm water and cool air
Nature seduces us with intoxicating keenness from below & above
We submerge within caresses of the wetness of memory and care
Knowing we will defend what exhilarates and shelter what we love

Today 's stiff muscles, & creaking joints present reminders
Of why keep up the assuaging motion under warmish water
thus far we are in truth, resolute, indomitable, birds of a feather
Yet we know well existential veracity: Pool Blather depends on
weather

The nature / nurture debate still continues its balancing act; one year its nurture the next its nature or a combination.
The "Expression of genetic via environmental impacts" is popular this year.

THE DEEP INSIDE

We can never quite disregard or be shorn
Of the needs with which we were born
Needs deep inside —

To be accepted as/is and concede
without judgment of a deed
or other needs deep inside —

To be beloved through the unquenchable
medium of touch-hungry bodies unstable
And enable that touch deep inside —

To be enfolded on another's pillowcase
And know the warmth of breast and embrace
And retrace the calm deep inside —

This is not validated empirical balm
But only a wad of meek wisdom
Wherefrom to touch a place deep inside…

Palm Springs architecture was "born mid-century," (i.e. 1950s) and as such, becomes one of the reasons that an epoch in a time past is mythologized as a more "perfect" period in history

GOOD OL' DAYS — MID CENTURY MODERN — PALM SPRINGS

We squirm through distorted memories — fleckless with naiveté
Born from our own cluelessness of those "innocent times" so gay
We suffer sun and wind & shun the sad distressing syndromes
of those who live within the dank paper shacks called "home".
Then close our minds eye & dream of the Magical "good ol' days"
When polio crippled and murdered little children without faze
Cigarette smoking & segregation were God's natural ways

Distorted desire returns us to memories of mid-century "innocence"
Whether by sadistic comfort or misshapen sensual non-'sense'
We crave a glimpse of the magical "good ol' days" we oft desired
Where a blind man's begging bowl might just as well say liar
And a believing mother's child enfolded in a jam-stained skirt
Looks acceptable with chronic need & vacant eyes no longer alert
scream "God's sake! Stop him – our *Priest's* the implausible pervert"

We imagine the 50s were a simpler time – 'innocent' - the days were dubbed
two-faced citizens worked "hard"- feigned 'morality' - belonged to service clubs.
Duplicitous neighbors "respected" the laws of racist police 'Billy Clubs'
While churched citizens sent 50 thousand teen-aged kids to perish in Korea
(Wherever the hell that is!) Then remember too the communist panacea?
A yapping Senator raped our constitution and rubbed our noses in stink
Instilled fear and claimed communists were making us Yankees all pink

While our Federal Bureau investigated – Academicians - Hollywood actors -
even as homosexual agents coveted J Edgar's lady shoe collections
His "secret files" composed to protect American virtue (and mindless jobs)
While megalomania McCarthy paranoia ran rampant in the Congress mob,
"black lists" circulated and devastated creative careers and did gleefully rob
those *who-would-be-different* attitudes left no doubt about their compliance
to un-thinking American ideals silently submitted to "innocent ideals" reliance

Domestic wife rape & child violence in the "good ol' days" was totally tolerable
Not prosecutable said 50s court, merely-purely a right of man label: acceptable.
Beating on wives and children was commonly considered "domestic discipline'
In the uncomplicated 50s — cops didn't react to "domestic discipline" as sin.
California said it's illegal to bring to court macho-men for spouse exploitation
(Man's mandate pronounced such indictment a form of sexual discrimination)
Only post "deplorable *Hippy 60s*" domestic violence labeled *criminal* allegation

Pending the ending of the barely endurable yet "magical 50s" decade
Demanding in all public facilities segregation enforced by 50s law aid
Durst we dare recall *Jim Crowe* mandated by fanciful Latin *de jure*
Before Civil Rights movement of 60s, bigots' flaunted racisms lure
In the 50s one could be screened for skin color and gender unafraid
These were tangible "Biblically ingrained" practices subsequently laid
In a world of 'whites only' and 'colored only' in the "good ol' days".

In the "magical 50s" Air Conditioning was a gleam in a Gatsbyesque venue
True, AC 's not green — takes tons of overindulgence & energy boo coos
then too, people die in heat waves! While we ponder, diseases pass in review
The good ol' days owned many brands of gasoline but no Federal Highways –
Today, we take the lacey racy Paved Fed highways for granted & by-the-way
getting from point A to point B in reasonable lines is no hocus pocus today .
in the 50s, not only did your car (if you owned one) get piteous gas-mileage, interstate travel was a nightmare of driving from NY to LA using local silage.

While our 50s "proper Americans" (aka – WASP men) bragged and puffed up
Their music was unbearably terribly misconceived copies of pre-made-setups
And parents resisted, even hated their children's "Black Music screw-ups":
Rock and Roll, Blues and Jazz — and even Elvis was measured mostly 'black'
Sans the existence of Face book and I Tunes, the mid-century mostly lacked
The hippest hipsters couldn't stay alongside. Yes, 50s Music in fact, lack
what downloaded music & *garage band* camp creations freely bivouac

During "magical 50s" drunk driving was common - a minor infraction – do tell
We could hardly expect one who was fall-down smashed to also drive well!
Homosexuality in Psychiatric Bible DMS listed as full-blown mental illness sells.
I'm not saying that there wasn't anything good about the "magical 50s" in fact
Good literature was written – J. D. Salinger, Tennessee Williams, Jack Kerouac,
I am saying the 50s were not a dream 'magical' time – (words to redact)
Not magical, not even simple. It's *hazardous* to our health & even moronic
To cast past, people, cultures, or certain times in history as idealized or iconic

We can, we must *appreciate the present for what it is*. Celebrate the NOW
and marvelous things available, indeed say splendid things about Tao:
(Tao Te Ching) the 'unspeakable' way or path... Communication, transportation, NOVA, NASA, gobbling Google, U tube TED talks, and electronic education
mind-blowing iPhone - IPad inventions Internet service of infinite information
look up new data 24/7 without a physical library or even a card-index
We now have astonishing access to novel entertainment media complex
There are good reasons why the past is the past. Take a breath! Relax!!!

If only we would re- mind and re-member: Be Here Now

HEROES of the dawn?

An additional thought about our beloved, selective and 'magical' recollection of history: Even though Jefferson is, in the minds of most Americans, one of our most adored and admired anti-religious Founding Fathers, he was a racist!

True, most modern historians excuse his racism and cruelty as a by-product of the times.

Also true – most historians attempt to square his famous rhetoric of liberty writing with his real life support for slavery by excusing this irreconcilable reality as an "artifact of his times" (Everyone was doing it!) But like other historical "ugly truths" the man who wrote (or plagiarized from French documents) the Declaration of Independence, which enshrined the "self-evident truth" - that all men were "created equal", was also a fervent buyer and seller of human beings.

While George Washington freed his slaves, Thomas Jefferson continued his personal enslavement 175 men and women on his Monticello estate. He sold them off – breaking up families — with an obvious indifference to the pain he caused.

With the traditional arrogance of British royalty he used his slave-profits to buy French wines and art.

Sally Hemming, his slave mistress, gave birth to his unacknowledged offspring, while he insisted that blacks were inferior "in body and mind" and that they "lacked basic human emotion."

So like other mythologized and/or defied historical figures (real or fictional) lets stop cloaking the past in ill-conceived courageous and/or superhuman fantasy. Jefferson like many of our most revered heroes was, among many other things, a brutal hypocrite.

Never enough said ... although it has been said "unhappy is the land that breeds no heroes" "NO!" Says Galileo, "Unhappy is the land that needs heroes!"

DEATH

"We are going to die, and that makes us the lucky ones. Most people are never going to die because they are never going to be born. The potential people who could have been here in my place but who will in fact never see the light of day outnumber the sand grains of Arabia. Certainly those unborn ghosts include greater poets than Keats, scientists greater than Newton. We know this because the set of possible people allowed by our DNA so massively exceeds the set of actual people. In the teeth of these stupefying odds it is you and I, in our ordinariness, that are here."

-Richard Dawkins

CONTEMPLATION OF DAWN

In the natural zest of early morn drenched in molecules of light
flourishing *Homo sapiens* arise Celebrating quietude and
65 million years of dawn's contemplative augmentation
Without twinge or the slightest doubt of how to salute a hero - is
madly driven

Today in the hush of early morning I seek evocative words
to describe how the morning photons take delight In compelling
such a solemn dark thought to vacate mind rooms and allow
the cheers of reflection while occupying the naissance space behind
my eyes

In the zest-filled early morning light the re-birth of life's essentials
reconfigure Just as the flowering vines twist to the sun *wise humans*
with predictive computers configure the next big-eyed – brain inkling
of *sapiens* appear hero-less next dawn with effortless Meditatio*n*
birthing the day

Notorious Night people believe the hero salutation. Sleeping through
the hush of day's new beginning omitting the brief colorful rushes &
wisps of air that whisper sacred epiphanies in early stillness
that energizes the stretch and yawns of waking to the splendor of
beautiful morning light & press into day the first pant of
creative exploit

In some far distant time, heroes were sought as respite from
vulnerable threat and throat cry tuned to show submission to the noir
monsters Today — lasers and LED lights ignite the dark
So that sleep eludes — first light is hushed Closed eyes and open
dry mouths snort our past addiction to heroes - lost in dawn's
brisk zest

Edwards Brothers Malloy
Oxnard, CA USA
November 22, 2013